The Spirit of Northern Italy

By Marco P. Zecchin

)(
An Image Center Book
Los Gatos, California

Image Center
P.O. Box 786
Los Gatos, California 95031
www.image-center.com

Front cover: Roadside Chapel, San Martino di Campagna - 1997

Dedicated to my daughter

Zoe Mia Stellina Zecchin

First Edition

ISBN 0-9746546-0-4

Printed in United States of America

CONTENTS

Acknowledgments

I believe that the creation of my art is a collaboration between the Spirit and myself. Our relationship is primal and has lead me though some difficult and joyous times to make me who I am today. Thank you.

There are many relationships that have influenced and guided me toward the creation of this book. First, I would like to thank my parents, Luciano Zecchin and Enes Della Santina Zecchin. In hopes of giving me their best advice in life, tried to dissuade me from taking up an artists life–they succeeded in inspiring me. I am grateful that they lived long enough to see and embrace my success. They also guided me to my Italian heritage. The exploration of which lies on every level in these photographs. Mary Kay Zecchin who encouraged and enabled me to follow my photographic path. My family in Italy, especially Daniela Zecchin. You accepted my eccentricities with grace and encouragement–*mille grazie!* Sally Redfield for showing me that through faith and patience dreams come true. Jean-Dominique Savelli, for your friendship and extraordinary skill in holding up the mirror and showing me the opportunities. My photographic mentor and friend, Morley Baer. Thank you for seeing something in me worth nurturing. The Baerly Masters, especially, Craig Barber, Kent Johns, Mark Nolan, Nanci Ori, and Tom Parker, who have kept Morley's light bright in his absence. To my many friends, patrons and supporters, the relationships that we have keeps me going behind the camera in wonder.

Introduction

The creative process is a prayer for understanding. The art work created is the evidence of that process.

With this belief firmly in hand, I follow the direction of some visceral, spiritual need. I find that this connection with my subject opens my eyes to its beauty—or at least its beauty revealed to me. It is the relationship of shared energies that makes the statement. Not the artist and not the subject alone but the connection (collaboration) the two have that transforms the craft into an artistic expression.

Like any relationship some magically appear with shocking familiarity, others mature slowly, requiring a trust be developed before revealing itself. Courage is required since the best of these relationships help reveal less than beautiful parts of ourselves. Courage to embrace and transmute these parts into extraordinary beauty. All relationships require compassion and faith that the engagement will ultimately help us understand ourselves, others, place and especially spirit, far better in the end.

The images I create are my evidence of this process.

The Spirit of Northern Italy

Through the window of the airplane, I was looking at the Alps but I did not see them. Leaving Italy and heading back to San Francisco, I was lost in my emotions. Returning to my Father's family home in Italy after twenty-six years and taking photographs had been my plan. The emotions I was feeling were strong. They were too be the first inkling of life's bigger plan for me. A plan that I would have to give myself over too and simply live. A plan that would return me to Italy in order to understand my Father's life, his influence on me and ultimately myself through photography.

My Father's family is from Venice. Our home in Maniago, sixty miles north east of Venice, has been in the family hundreds of years. In the centuries since the house was built little had changed. While in the 1800's it was the center of the family's agricultural businesses, today it is just a summer residence. The stone walls not easily heated in the bitter winters at the foot of the Alps, make for a wonderful refuge in the heat of *ferragosto*, the summer holidays.

I was twelve in 1967 when we last visited Italy, a summer trip filled with joy, laughter and family. The house was still a working farm in those days, with chickens to chase and cows to torment. The machinery for working the land, wooden and weathered, were garaged in the surrounding outbuildings. The sound of them leaving for the fields around the village, woke me most mornings. An earthy cacophony of wagon wheels grinding and popping on pavement mixed with barked directions and whistles the farm hands gave the horses pulling their burden.

The gathering place for the family was a large room furnished with a wood stove, small breakfast table that doubled as a food preparation surface and a long dining room table. Breakfast was eaten individually at the '50's style metal edged laminate table, as we trickled down from the bedrooms each morning. The family came together at lunch and dinner around the long dining room table, lingering after each meal in conversation and laughter. In one corner of the room, a two tiered wash basin, decorated with faucet mouthed cherubic faces, fascinated me. It's obsolescence with indoor plumbing had relegated it to being the telephone's residence with tattered address books, note pads and pencils for company. The loggia on the second floor, was the central room of a suite of four bedrooms. It was filled with dark furniture and even darker faced portraits. Those portraits terrorized me as I ran out of my bedroom and down the hall to the light and safety of the family room. Can anything scare a twelve year old more than the stern face of authority?

When I returned, twenty-six years later, the chickens and cows along with the farm lands were gone. Community gas lines brought a new three burner range and heater to replace the wood stove in the kitchen but everything else remained the same. On this visit, after reacquainting ourselves, my relatives gave us a couple of days alone in the house and so I wandered looking for photographs. My reverberating footsteps echoed those of my childhood. Slowly I visited all the rooms running my fingers along the surfaces and taking in the smells of the old house. I was lost in my memories. Trying to find the feeling of the place so that I could photograph it was not the problem. My problem was that I was paralyzed due to the intensity of the feelings I found there.

I am an architectural photographer. Photographing homes and buildings had been my specialty for eight years at that point. Learning to photograph by feeling was drilled in by my mentor, Morley Baer.

Stories of his Grandmother in Ohio reminding him that whatever he did he needed to do "mit feeling," was a large part of his photographic lesson plan. It was not an easy lesson to learn in my thirty's. Life tends to create barriers to protect one from feeling too much. I certainly was guilty of that. When it happened and with what image I cannot pinpoint. Allowing my feelings to guide me to an image and just responding to it, was a quiet epiphany. Hidden in years of practice that made the process of making photographs disappear from my consciousness.

Being reminded that I only had a day left at the house, shook me from my paralysis and I started taking photographs.

How I photograph can be best described by the example of how a dowser finds water. Giving up to my feelings the camera in my hand becomes a divining rod. Through it I follow an invisible thread of energy to an image. In the house, filled with memories, I was overwhelmed. Tears and nausea made slow work of my usual expeditious pace. Even the subsequent visit to family in Venice, that same overpowering feelings continued. Visiting Torcello, an outer island in the Venetian lagoon that I had not visited as a child, I was allowed a respite and photographed in peace.

On the flight home, turned completely to the airplane's window, I was not enjoying the view of the Alps, I was hiding. Hiding the tears and quivering breath that I could not stop. The confrontation of my joyful childhood memories in Italy, untouched by time and the subsequent years of unresolved rebellion from my Father, came rushing in—chaotic and bewildering.

The weeks and months that followed my return didn't bring much relief. In my emotional mess I lashed out and pointed fingers at others for my state. During this time one helpful thought was shared with me—when you point a finger at others there are three pointing back. The confusion within me had to be dealt with. Blaming others was pointless. The photographs that I had taken during the visit felt different and were filled "mit feeling." These images told me that photography would help me focus and sort through my turmoil. Returning to my family home in Italy became an imperative.

Two years later I did return. Wanting to avail me of her local knowledge, and get to know each other after twenty-six years, my Cousin Daniela asked me what it was that I wanted to photograph. I had to say that I hadn't a clue, that what I needed to photograph would make itself known.

I had consciously stopped listening to my Father as a teenager but the names I saw on the map I used to organize my visit, resonated. Spilimbergo, Frisanco, Barcis, Conegliano, Chimolais, Longarone, Cortina d'Ampezzo, Treviso and always Venezia. Visiting each town, the stories my Father told of his youth started to have meaning. The layers of memories began to separate.

We drove, camera in the trunk, till I sensed an energetic thread. It wasn't long before we came to a village called Villanova—a corner in the road. Slowing to negotiate it, I saw the crumbling wall kept upright by logs leaned into the bulges. I followed the wall, covered by vines that crept onto an ornate iron gate at its opening. I slowed further. A statue of a child looking toward the mountains stood atop the opposing column. A quick glance through the filigree lattice of the gate revealed a grassy track leading to the woods beyond. The spirit doesn't speak in loud gestures, not even in Italy. I drove on. But a niggling feeling arose. Was it the crumbling wall, the gate, the vine, the statue or jet lag that convinced me to turn my car around, I do not know? But I did.

Progress in life has its mile markers and sign posts, more easily seen when looking back. Driving back over that road I had just taken I felt the adage, "hindsight is 20/20," taking form.

Returning, I was able to see over the wall what I could not see driving from the opposite direction. A gleaming grand arch, hit by the sun as the clouds were dissipating, was the apex of a facade of arched windows. I stopped short of the entry, climbed out of the car and walked towards the gate. Through it, stately and quiet, recently restored and white washed, was the early eighteenth century villa known as Villa Marini. In the yard brightly colored plastic children's toys spoke to an ordinary family life lived amidst history.

In familiar fashion, I retrieved my camera from the car and with practiced hands set up and took a photograph of a building. How could I continue hiding from the fact that I had been mentored by an architectural photographer, became an architectural photographer, and here, in my art, was speaking in the voice of architecture, without recognizing the influence my Father, an Architect, had on my life? In this moment of confluence, my thoughts and feelings did not boil and tumble. Instead, a feeling of clarity and solidity arose. Was this the solid ground I was trying to uncover?

With this feeling as my guide, I began looking for and photographing the old buildings of the area. In those towns and villages that were the settings for my Father's stories, I found the churches, roadside chapels and mausoleums, in their honor of the spirit–the sacred, and the villas, in their excess–the profane.

In them I also found a man's life.

Venezia, was my Father's birthplace. He spoke of it with pride and love. His identity throughout his life was based on his being a Venetian. As a child, it was my playground, my Disneyland. No cars to worry about. Vendors along the quay of the Grand Canal and the Rialto offering toys and trinkets that I would point out, eliciting a scoff from whichever adult was accompanying us. Running through the pigeons in Piazza San Marco, the flutter of wings and the screams of whomever was tormented by a bird flying too close, music to a twelve year olds ears.

I have never had the feeling of homecoming like I experience in Venice. It is a mystery how this city magically cradles me in the comfort of familiarity. Have I lived there before or is it just a melange of childhood memories, my Father's stories and my own studies of Venetian history that are subconsciously playing a game with me? If one can feel history, I feel it in the pavement of Venice. In the maze of calle, the Venetian streets, the question, "who has stepped on these stones?", electrifies each step I take.

To photograph Venice, I strip down my camera bag to the bare essentials but its weight still can dictate where I stop to photograph. Is it the energetic thread of this place that reveals it's photographs to me or the aching shoulder that speaks louder? Remaining connected to the thread while hurting, evades me. My camera bag at times feeling like Sisyphus's stone. Does it carry a tool to my understanding or simply another piece of baggage I need to shed? I have one rule in Venice–get lost! But my familiarity with the city, increasing with each visit, makes this harder to do. At least harder to do without going further into the maze carrying my burden.

Over the years, the Venetian calle and sottoporticci, churches and palazzi, canals and lagoon have become a metaphoric maze to mine my shadows. I don't remember when I started looking at my psychological shadows but it was in Venice that I started noticing them in my photographs. Are they simply detached graphic forms, like Peter Pan's shadow that needs sewing to something real, do they hold some deeper meaning or is it all just trite cliché? Whichever is irrelevant! Whatever it takes to be in touch with myself and my own ability to create, is valid. Making photographs through which I can pass beyond the simple shades of gray, into my own light and shadow, the blessing.

Like a patient parent, loving friend, or high paid psychologist, Venice, as her monicker *La Serenissima* proclaims, allows me to explore myself in serenity. Of course family life, even in Venice, isn't always serene. My Uncle accompanies me many afternoons, wanting to be in his nephews company and sharing our mutual love of photography. He had been my Father's best friend and became part of the family by marrying his youngest sister. He is a reservoir of stories and adventures he had with my Father, so I pay attention when he speaks but he mumbles in a dialect I am familiar but not comfortable with and he has difficulty walking in silence. Being open to the energetic thread that I struggle with in Venice, is virtually impossible in my Uncle's company. Not wanting to seem rude or ungrateful, I stew in my frustration.

One particular day passing through Campo San Polo, stewing, we came upon two of my Uncle's friends. In Venice, there are traditions that have survived the centuries. Maybe not with the flourish it once had but the courtly bow still exists. Having been a few paces behind, I took his arresting gesture as an opportunity of turning down a side calle–I ditched my Uncle! Out of his sight, I raced through this unknown part of town to make good my escape. I pressed on, comfort-

able knowing he would excuse my lack of courtly sensibilities by simply stating *"Americano!"* with a shrug, but escape was not too be. The calle came to an end. In my stunned disbelief or hope in finding some hidden escape, I pressed on to the private door of the Palazzo that was the end. In my resignation, I turned to face the consequences of my action. In that acceptance of my fate, *La Serenissima* presented me with an exquisite view of three columns that flanked the water entrance to this Palazzo. I have no idea if the reason I was given this image was to provide me an excuse for ditching my Uncle or an opportunity to throw my dark cloth over my camera and myself and magically disappear. I have never learned the incantation for vanishing but the lesson of facing my choice did not escape me–nor did the photograph.

During the past decade of visiting Italy, the experiences and photographs of my family home in Maniago, the old villas and churches, calli and canali, I shared with my Father. The common ground we found in these conversations formed the gentler relationship that I lovingly carry now in his absence. These photographs help me remember my families history and my Father's life through the stories they hold. Remembering and accepting, as a part of who I am, the spirit of northern Italy and the family that came from it.

Family Home

Window Detail, Maniago - 1993

Family Loggia, Maniago - 1993

13

Family Kitchen II, Maniago - 1993

Family Kitchen I, Maniago - 1993

Wash basin, Maniago - 1993

Venezia

Sottoportico, Venice - 1995

San Marco Back Door, Venice - 1995

Ramo Moro Lin, Venice - 1997

Parrocchia di San Salvador, Venice - 1995

21

Ramo Berziza, Venice - 1995

Greek Orthodox Canal Entry, Venice - 1995

Archaeological Wall, Torcello, Venice - 1993

Boca de la Verita, Torcello, Venice - 1993

27

Roman Bridge, Torcello, Venice - 1993

Calle Dei Botteri, Venice - 1995

29

Garden Figures, Torcello, Venice - 1993

Window Detail, Venice - 1997

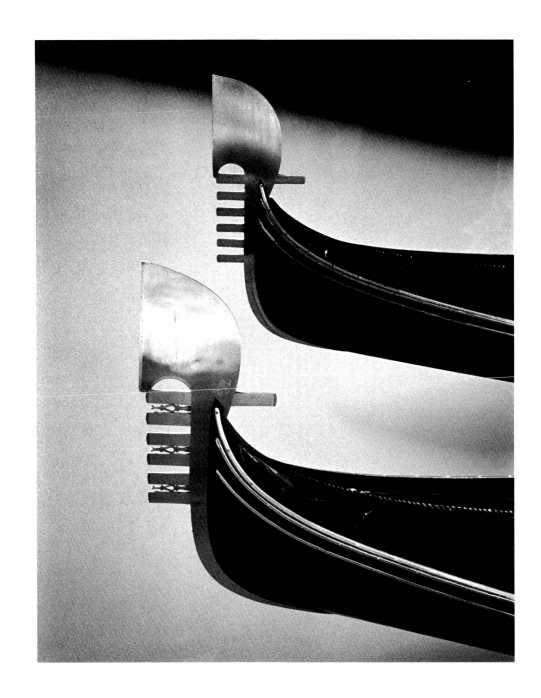

31

Gondolas, Venice - 1998

Sacred and Profane

Villa Marini, Villanova - 1993

Villa Giustiniani, Portobuffole - 1995

Family Mausoleum, Marinella - 1995

Villa Manin, Passariani - 1995

Roadside Chapel I, Castelle di Monfamo - 1997

Villa and Oratorio, Battaglia Terme - 1995

Roadside Chapel II, Castelle di Monfamo - 1997

Roadside Chapel, San Martino di Campagna - 1997

Roadside Chapel I, Bibione - 1995

Roadside Chapel II, Bibione - 1995

43

Villa Varda Chapel II, Brugnera - 1995

Villa Varda Chapel I, Brugnera - 1995

Villa Varda Mausoleum, Brugnera - 1995

47 | *Villa Varda Out Building II, Brugnera - 1997*

Villa Varda Out Building I, Brugnera - 1995

Villa Varda Tower, Brugnera - 1997

Centurion Tree, Cordignano - 1997

51 | *Per i Caduti Alpini, San Leonardo - 1997*

Dedication, Bresanone - 2002

54

Duomo, Gemona - 1995

Noncello River, Cordenons - 2002

Fiume Reghena, Sesto al Reghena - 1997

57

Field Road, Cordenons - 2002

List of Plates and Negative Numbers

1. Window Detail, Maniago - 1993 - (930512-I)
2. Family Loggia, Maniago - 1993 - (930517-C)
3. Family Kitchen II, Maniago - 1993 - (930516-C)
4. Family Kitchen I, Maniago - 1993 - (930516-B)
5. Wash basin, Maniago - 1993 - (930516-A)
6. Sottoportico, Venice - 1995 - (950617-C)
7. San Marco Back Door, Venice - 1995 - (950619-B)
8. Ramo Moro Lin, Venice - 1997 - (971013-C)
9. Parrocchia di San Salvador, Venice - 1995 - (950619-A)
10. Corte Amaltea, Venice - 1997 - (971013-B)
11. Ramo Berziza, Venice - 1995 - (950620-C)
12. Greek Orthodox Canal Entry, Venice - 1995 - (950619-C)
13. Bridge and Gondola, Venice - 1997 - (971013-D)
14. Archeological Wall, Torcello, Venice - 1993 - (930518-B)
15. Boca de la Verita, Torcello, Venice - 1993 - (930518-A)
16. Roman Bridge, Torcello, Venice - 1993 - (930518-D)
17. Calle Dei Botteri, Venice - 1995 - (950617-A)
18. Garden Figures, Torcello, Venice - 1993 - (930518-C)
19. Window Detail, Venice - 1997 - (971011-B)
20. Gondolas, Venice - 1998 - (981015-A)
21. Villa Marini, Villanova - 1995 - (950615-C)
22. Villa Manin, Passariani - 1995 - (950605-C)
23. Villa Giustiniani, Portobuffole - 1995 - (950615-D)
24. Family Mausoleum, Marinella - 1995 - (950614-B)
25. Roadside Chapel I, Castelle di Monfamo - 1997 - (971012 A)
26. Villa and Oratorio, Battaglia Terme - 1995 - (950618-A)
27. Roadside Chapel II, Castelle di Monfamo - 1997 - (971012-C)
28. Roadside Chapel, San Martino di Campagna - 1997 - (971008-E)
29. Roadside Chapel I, Bibione - 1995 - (950603-B)
30. Roadside Chapel II, Bibione - 1995 - (950603-A)
31. Ancient Foundation, Sesto al Reghena - 1995 - (950601-B)
32. Villa Varda Chapel II, Brugnera - 1995 - (950605-P)
33. Villa Varda Chapel I, Brugnera - 1995 - (950605-O)
34. Villa Varda Mausoleum, Brugnera - 1995 - (950605-Q)
35. Villa Varda Out Building II, Brugnera - 1997 - (971002-D)
36. Villa Varda Out Building I, Brugnera - 1995 - (950605-M)
37. Villa Varda Tower, Brugnera - 1997 - (971002-C)
38. Centurion Tree, Cordignano - 1997 - (971002-G)
39. Per i Caduti Alpini, San Leonardo - 1997 - (971008-D)
40. Roadside Sanctuary, Bresanone - 2002 - (021023-F)
42. Dedication, Bresanone - 2002 - (021023-E)
43. Duomo, Gemona - 1995 - (950609-A)
44. Noncello River, Cordenons - 2002 - (021017-C)
45. Fiume Reghena, Sesto al Reghena - 1997 - (971006-A)
46. Field Road, Cordenons - 2002 - (021018-A)

Patrons Page

Diamond Legacy Patron

W. Kent Johns

Thomas Parker

Mary Kay and Zoe Zecchin

Platinum Legacy Patron

DeCarolis Design & Marketing

Michelle Corbit and Teo Torres Machacek

Amelia Redfield

Gold Legacy Patron

Thomas Gary Howard and Tess Cain

Rich Ferrari

Eric and Polly Fox

Robert Maddox and Uwe Mueller

Tom Malone

Jeff Redman

Jenny and Lex Speal

Silver Legacy Patron

Liz Welsh Abad and Jose M. Abad

Keith Brauneis

Anita and Larry Fein

David and Betsy Fullagar

Dwight and Shannon Grissom

Denise Henderson

Wanda Kownacki

Rebecca Love

Joe and Elizabeth Mandato

Manu

Mark and Zita Nolan

David Pace and Diane Jonte-Pace

Kathy De La Torre

Dave, Wendy, Makenna and Danielle Vis

Jack and Beverly Waltman

Curtis Wilson

Patricia Ann Wyatt and Stephanie Demos

Valerie J. Young